Rookie
Read-About®
Holidays

Thanksgiving

by Lisa M. Herrington

Content Consultants
Plimoth Plantation, Plymouth, Massachusetts

Carrie A. Bell, MST Visual Arts — All Grades
Julia A. Stark Elementary School, Stamford, Connecticut

Reading Consultant
Jeanne M. Clidas, Ph.D.
Reading Specialist

Children's Press®
An Imprint of Scholastic Inc.
New York Toronto London Auckland Sydney
Mexico City New Delhi Hong Kong
Danbury, Connecticut

Library of Congress Cataloging-in-Publication Data
Herrington, Lisa M.
  Thanksgiving / by Lisa M. Herrington.
    pages cm. — (Rookie read-about holidays)
  Includes index.
  ISBN 978-0-531-27206-0 (library binding) — ISBN 978-0-531-27356-2 (pbk.)
  1. Thanksgiving Day—Juvenile literature. I. Title.

  GT4975H48 2013
  394.2649—dc23   2013014851

Produced by Spooky Cheetah Press

© 2014 by Scholastic Inc.

Printed in China 62

SCHOLASTIC, CHILDREN'S PRESS, ROOKIE READ-ABOUT®, and associated logos
are trademarks and/or registered trademarks of Scholastic Inc.

1 2 3 4 5 6 7 8 9 10 R 23 22 21 20 19 18 17 16 15 14

Photographs © 2014: Adam Chinitz: 28; Louise Gardner: 7; Media Bakery/SW
Productions: 23, 31 bottom; Plimoth Plantation: cover, 12, 15, 16, 19, 30, 31 center
bottom; Shutterstock, Inc./Lev Radin: 20; Superstock, Inc.: 24 (Ariel Skelley/
Blend Images), 27 (Belinda Images), 4, 31 top (Cusp); The Granger Collection: 8;
Thinkstock/iStockphoto: 3 top, 3 bottom, 31 center top; XNR Productions: 11.

Table of Contents

A Day of Thanks **5**

How It Began **9**

Thanksgiving Today **21**

Let's Celebrate! 28

Show What You Know! 30

Glossary 31

Index 32

Facts for Now 32

About the Author 32

4

A Day of Thanks

Fall is here! The turkey and pumpkin pie are ready to eat. Families are gathered. It is time to celebrate Thanksgiving!

Thanksgiving falls on a different date in November from year to year.

Each year, Thanksgiving takes place on the fourth Thursday in November. On this day, families sit down to enjoy a **feast** and give thanks.

FAST FACT!

In 1863, President Abraham Lincoln made Thanksgiving a holiday for the whole country.

NOVEMBER

SUNDAY	MONDAY	TUESDAY	WEDNESDAY	THURSDAY	FRIDAY	SATURDAY
						1
2	3	4	5	6	7	8
9	10	11	12	13	14	15
16	17	18	19	20	21	22
23	24	25	26	27	28	29
30						

7

How It Began

In September 1620, a group of people left England for North America. We call them the **Pilgrims**. They wanted to start a new life in a new land.

The Pilgrims sailed aboard a ship called the *Mayflower*.

9

It took the Pilgrims two months to reach North America.

The Pilgrims arrived in North America. They settled in Plymouth, in what is now Massachusetts.

FAST FACT!

There were 102 passengers crowded aboard the *Mayflower*.

10

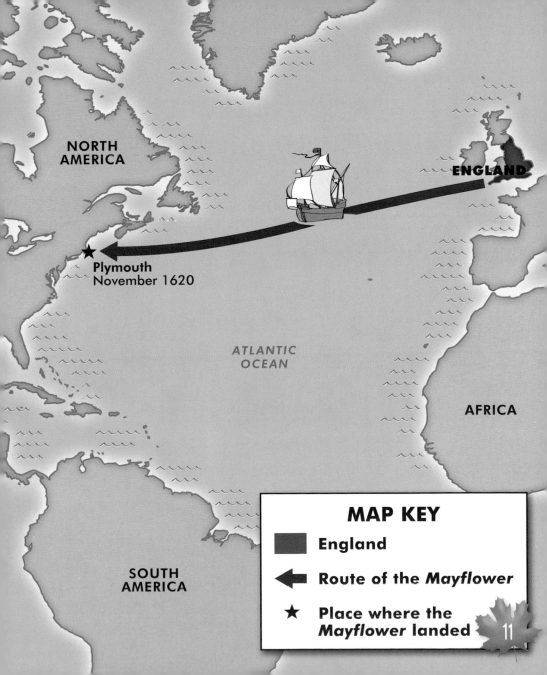

NORTH
AMERICA

ENGLAND

Plymouth
November 1620

ATLANTIC
OCEAN

AFRICA

SOUTH
AMERICA

MAP KEY

England

Route of the *Mayflower*

★ Place where the
Mayflower landed

11

The Pilgrims started to build their homes. The first winter was very cold and hard. There was not enough food. Many of the Pilgrims got sick or died.

The Pilgrims worked hard to survive in their new land.

Native Americans were already living on the land when the Pilgrims arrived. The Wampanoag (wahm-pah-NOH-ahg) people lived in the area. They showed the Pilgrims how to fish and hunt.

FAST FACT!

A Wampanoag man named Squanto helped the Pilgrims survive.

The Wampanoag people taught the Pilgrims which plants were safe to eat. They also taught the Pilgrims how to plant corn using fish to make the soil richer.

This photo shows how Squanto taught the Pilgrims to plant corn.

In the fall of 1621, the Pilgrims had plenty of food. They wanted to celebrate their **harvest**. They held a big feast. The Wampanoag people joined them. Their celebration became known as the first Thanksgiving.

Some foods served at the feast probably included corn, deer meat, and fowl, such as duck.

Thanksgiving Today

People celebrate Thanksgiving in many ways. There are parades that take place on Thanksgiving Day. The most famous is the Macy's Thanksgiving Day Parade in New York City.

The Macy's parade is known for its huge balloons of popular characters.

Some people collect food for the poor on Thanksgiving. They also **volunteer** to serve meals to people in need. They see Thanksgiving as a time to help others.

This family is serving a Thanksgiving meal to the needy.

Some people spend Thanksgiving playing or watching football. Kids often make Thanksgiving crafts to decorate their homes.

This family is playing a game of touch football.

No matter what people are doing, they are thankful to be with their family and friends on this special day. How will *you* celebrate Thanksgiving?

Gobble, gobble! People in the United States eat about 46 million turkeys on Thanksgiving.

Make a Thankful Tree

What You'll Need

- Posterboard or white paper
- Brown paint
- Red, yellow, and orange construction paper
- Pencil
- Glue
- Crayons or markers

Directions

1. Paint a brown tree trunk on the poster board. Start by painting a big letter Y for the trunk and two branches. Then connect more branches to the tree by painting wavy lines from the trunk and branches.

2. Tear off pieces of red, yellow, and orange paper to make leaves.

3. Think about what you are thankful for. Use the pencil or marker to write it on a leaf. Then ask your family members what they are thankful for. Write each person's response on a leaf. Glue the leaves to your thankful tree.

4. Now use the crayons or markers to decorate the background of your picture with scenes from fall. You might include grass, a sky, clouds, pumpkins, and fallen leaves. Use your creativity and add whatever you'd like to make your Thanksgiving picture complete!

The First Thanksgiving

Look at the photo and imagine you are a reporter at the first Thanksgiving feast.

- *Who* was there?
- *What* was being celebrated?
- *Where* was it celebrated?
- *When* was it celebrated?
- *Why* was it being celebrated?
- *How* was it being celebrated?

Thanksgiving: Then and Now

- Compare the first Thanksgiving feast with how we celebrate Thanksgiving today.
- Describe one way the two are alike.

Glossary

feast (feest): a big meal for a special occasion

harvest (HAR-vist): crops that are gathered

Pilgrims (PIL-gruhms): the group of people who left England for North America in 1620

volunteer (vol-uhn-TIHR): to do a job without pay

Index

England 9

feast 6, 18

food 5, 13, 18, 22, 26

football 25

harvest 18

Lincoln, Abraham 6

Mayflower 10

parades 21

Pilgrims 9–18

Plymouth,
   Massachusetts 10

Squanto 14

turkey 5, 26

volunteer 22

Wampanoag people
   14, 17, 18

Facts for Now

Visit this Scholastic Web site for more information on Thanksgiving:
www.factsfornow.scholastic.com
Enter the keyword **Thanksgiving**

About the Author

Lisa M. Herrington is a freelance writer and editor. Lisa lives in
Trumbull, Connecticut, with her husband, Ryan, and her daughter,
Caroline. She is thankful for her many wonderful Thanksgivings with
her family, especially those with her grandparents. She dedicates this
book to them.